PROPHETIC FIRE & GLORY

By

PHILLIP RICH

EKKLISIA PROPHETIC APOSTOLIC MINISTRIES, INC.

PUBLISHED BY EKKLISIA MINISTRIES

Copyright 2006 A. D.

All rights reserved under International Copyright law. No part of this publication may be reproduced, stored in a retrieval system, or transmitted, in whole or in part, in any form or by any means, electronic, mechanical, photocopying, recording or otherwise, without the prior express consent of the publisher. All scripture is the Kings James Version unless otherwise stated. All rights reserved.

Take note that the name satan is not capitalized. We choose not to acknowledge him, even to the point of violating grammatical rules.

Table of Contents

Introduction 1

Seven Facts About Prophetic Fire 8

How to Enter the Fire & the Glory 24

Sow Prayer / Reap Fire 31

Romancing the Flame 45

House of Fire / House of Glory 55

- Prophetic Fire & Glory -

Introduction

Acts 2:17-19; *"And it shall come to pass in the last days, saith God, I will pour out of my Spirit upon all flesh: and <u>your</u> sons and your daughters shall <u>prophesy</u>, and <u>your</u> young men shall see visions, and <u>your</u> old men shall dream dreams: And on <u>my</u> servants and on <u>my</u> handmaidens I will pour out in those days of my Spirit; and they shall <u>prophesy</u>: And I will shew wonders in heaven above, and signs in the earth beneath; blood, and fire, and vapour of smoke:"*

This prophecy was first given by Joel in Joel 2. On the day of Pentecost, the Lord released the understanding of that prophecy when Peter got up and began to bring it forth. The full fulfillment of it has not happened yet. I have seen churches come under the fire of God, under the anointing of the Lord. But we have not yet seen the entire world covered by the outpouring of the Spirit. Yet, we know we are in the season of fulfillment, in the beginning stages of it.

The prophecy says that there will be signs and wonders. It mentions blood, fire and vapor of smoke. When we begin to look at this we know that it isn't just a few signs and wonders that will happen, any more than the outpouring of the Holy Spirit means that a little bit of rain is going to fall.

If God says He is going to show blood, fire and vapor of smoke we are going to have to look in the Spirit at the revelation of something that He is going to show. If He is going to show blood, it means He is going to reveal a revelation of the blood of Jesus in all the earth.

- Prophetic Fire & Glory -

I believe there is going to be a revelation of the sanctifying fire of God. There are two types of spiritual fire: zeal and desire. The Word says that the zeal of God has consumed me. Zeal means you are fired up, enthusiastic. With the zeal comes a burning desire. We will look at a burning zeal and a burning desire. They come with the outpouring of the Spirit, by the way.

There is a zeal for God. Have you ever had a zeal for God? You were so hungry you couldn't get enough of Him. You wanted to pray, get in the Word, be with God, press into God. When the zeal for the things of God is fully engaged in your spirit then God begins to release in you the zeal of God. The zeal of God is to win the world to Jesus Christ. God is zealous to evangelize the world. You can never have the zeal of God until you have the zeal for God. You have to be zealous to be with Him, to know Him, to be intimate with Him. When that has had its full work in you, He will transfer to you (by being with Him) the zeal of God, which is soul winning and mass world evangelism. Have you ever been intimate with God and all of a sudden felt a love that God put in your heart for the world, a love to win somebody to Jesus Christ?

Smoke is a type of the movement of the Spirit. The Holy Spirit is going to do an awesome work in the earth.
We are going to see the revelations of blood, fire and vapor of smoke in these hours. It is being released already, not sometime in the future.

The Lord said He was going to pour out His Spirit upon all flesh. Then He mentions your sons and your daughters. "*Your*" means the outpouring is connected with people, with flesh. It means that the people we love will begin to prophesy.

This first mention of prophecy is important for us to understand. I believe it is connected with the prophecy of scripture. Prophecy can never really be powerful in you until the Word of God is powerful in you. 2 Peter 1 talks about our having a more sure word of prophecy.

2 Peter 1:19; *"We have also a more sure word of prophecy; whereunto ye do well that ye take heed, as unto a light that shineth in a dark place, until the day dawn, and the day star arise in your hearts:"*

Jesus is the Living Word, the Daystar.

2 Peter 1:20-21; *"Knowing this first, that no prophecy of the scripture is of any private interpretation. For the prophecy came not in old time by the will of man: but holy men of God spake as they were <u>moved</u> by the Holy Ghost."*

If you don't have an unction, you can't function. If the Holy Ghost is not moving you, quit moving. If He is not speaking, don't you speak. There are people who think they can prophesy whatever they want and somehow God is going to bring it to pass. He never said He would confirm <u>your</u> word with signs following. He said He would confirm His Word. When He gives you a revelation, when He speaks a word from His Word to you and you speak what He is speaking He will back His Word, His movement, and His revelation. He doesn't have to back what you say.

Years ago I knew a prophet who felt that because he had the gift, he could prophesy just anything he wanted and God would back it up. What a fallacy. We are supposed to be mouthpieces for God. We are not directing God's mouth, He is directing ours. That is why I tell people, if I am not getting anything from God then I am not saying anything. If He gives me something I will give it. If He doesn't give me something there is nothing else worth saying. Only what He gives is important. What He does and what He says produces fruit that is lasting. What I do and what I say is for the moment and it is gone. Lasting fruit comes from God.

The first prophecy mentioned in Acts 2, the one connected to your sons and your daughters, is the prophecy of scripture because the Word of God is what transformed them. If you stay in the Word of God and get a revelation of it, it will change you. It will transform you from *your sons and your daughters* to *my servants and my handmaidens*.

As you speak the revelation you are transformed from someone who is owned by flesh. When you say *"my sons and my daughters"* you are speaking about someone who belongs to you, flesh connected to you.

But when God says my sons and my daughters He is talking about someone who has been transformed from flesh into something supernatural, into something extraordinary. The prophecy of scripture is prophesying the revelation of the Word.

One of the scriptural revelations that will change you is *"I am a new creature in Christ. Old things have passed away behold all things have become new."*[1] I can get a revelation of this and begin to prophesy, *"I am a new creature. The old things have passed away. All the new things have come. I am no longer as I used to be. I used to be a sinner but now I am saved by grace."* While I am prophesying it, the next thing happens. It is called dreams and visions.

Start speaking out the revelation of the Word of God and you will start seeing in the realm of the Spirit. Acts 2:17 says you will start seeing visions and dreams.

Now let's look at how a revelation of the Word of God will produce visions and dreams.

1 Samuel 3:1; "And the child Samuel ministered unto the LORD before Eli. And the word of the LORD was precious in those days; there was no open vision."

"Precious" is translated as scarce, hard to come by. What makes a precious stone precious is that there are not very many of them. The more something is scarce and hard to come by, the more precious it is.

There was very little revelation of the Word of God. Because there wasn't much revelation, there was no open vision. If my vision is separate from the Word of God, it is dangerous. If I am never in the Word of God,

---

[1] 2 Corinthians 5:17

never coming up with a revelation from the Word of God, never listen to preaching and teaching, never sharing scripture but I am always seeing something in the spirit you had better doubt what I am seeing.

Vision is supposed to come because of illumination. If you enter a room late at night and there were no lights on, and no light coming in through windows there would be very little, if any, vision. With no illumination there is little vision.

Psalms 119:130; *"The entrance of thy words giveth light; it giveth understanding unto the simple."*

The Word of God brings light. Where there is light, there is sight. Where there is spiritual light, there is spiritual sight. If you are seeing something and God's Word did not illuminate it to you, did not reveal it to you and it is not backed up by the Word of God, not connected to the Word of God then get rid of that thing as fast as you can.

One of the things we teach in the School of the Prophets[2] is how not to be a granola Christian – a fruit, nut or flake. If you are not grounded in the Word of God, then how do you know if what you are picking up is from God? God's Word regulates the whole thing. The way you know you are on the right track is from the Word of God. The way you know you are hearing the right voice is that it is from the Word of God.

The Bible says there are many voices and all of them have a reason for speaking things. Many of those voices, though, are deceptive. They sound like angels of light and can even quote scriptures. The devil quoted scriptures when Jesus was being tempted in the desert. He didn't read Him something out of the newspaper or a magazine. He quoted scripture and, of course, he quoted them wrong, leaving out certain things and adding other things. If you don't know the Word, you won't know the difference.

---

[2] The School of the Prophets is a four-year course that covers moving in the prophetic as well as Christian character and spiritual growth. This course is available as a correspondence course. Visit our website at www.ekklisiaministries.com.

So, we see that sight comes because of light. The light we are talking about is the light of the Word. The prophecy of scripture is the Word illuminated, brought forth by the Spirit of God.

Now let's return to Acts 2 to see the next thing about prophecy. Remember the first time we saw prophecy, the sons and daughters were going to do it and visions and dreams would accompany it.

Acts 2:18; *"And on my servants and on my handmaidens I will pour out in those days of my Spirit; and they shall prophesy:"*

Notice, there has been a transformation. Would you like for God to call you His servant or His handmaiden? Get enough Word in you and start prophesying what He is saying, get a revelation of the Word and the Lord will start coming to you saying, *"My servant. My handmaiden."*

This second mention of prophecy shall bring about a different thing than the first one. The first prophesying brought about sight in the Spirit. This second prophesying is the prophesying of visions and dreams that came because of the prophecy of scripture. So, the sons and daughters will be prophesying their dreams and visions that are based upon the Word.

When they start prophesying their dreams and visions look at what happens.

Acts 2:19; *"And I will shew wonders in heaven above, and signs in the earth beneath; blood, and fire, and vapour of smoke:"*

They start off by prophesying scripture and get changed from our sons and daughters to His servants and handmaidens. Then they get another outpouring of the Spirit and start prophesying the dreams and visions they saw because of the prophecy of scripture. As they are prophesying the dreams and visions God says, *"I am going to show signs and I am going to show wonders."*

The signs and wonders are connected to the dreams and visions they were prophesying. We will be prophesying signs and wonders and the Lord will confirm them because that is what He is revealing. Whatever He reveals, He heals. Whatever He speaks, He confirms it. He said, *"I am not a man that I should lie. If I said it, I will do it."*[3]

We are coming back to the Word of God and finding that every answer is there. We knew it was but now we are finding it out. We need the prophetic and the apostolic to help unveil it to us so we can enter it for ourselves.

---

[3] Numbers 23:19

Seven Facts About Prophetic Fire

This chapter will deal with seven facts about prophetic fire that will take you into the new day that you desire in God.

CONSUMING FIRE

We are going to connect consuming fire to the voice of God and the speaking of God. We know that as the prophetic.

Hebrews 12:25; *"See that ye refuse not him that <u>speaketh</u>. For if they escaped not who refused him that spake on earth, much more shall not we escape, if we turn away from him that <u>speaketh</u> from heaven:"*

See that ye refuse not him that speaketh is referring to God. Anytime a prophecy comes forth it is because God is saying something. He speaks many times to people who pick it up and repeat it. The Bible tells us that holy men of old spoke as they were moved by the Holy Ghost.[4] They received something and therefore could give something. We believe that unless you receive something from God, you cannot give anything. *"Silver and gold have I not, but such as I have give I to thee."*[5] If you don't have anything spiritual, you can't give anything spiritual. If God isn't speaking, we shouldn't speak. If He is silent, we should be silent. If He is saying something, we should say something.

---

[4] 2 Peter 1:21
[5] Acts 3:6

Hebrews 12:26; *"Whose voice then shook the earth: but now he hath promised, saying, Yet once more I shake not the earth only, but also heaven."*

"Voice" is related to the word *"speaketh"* but is a little different. The Greek word for *"voice"* is *fo-nay* and is where we get our word telephone. When you study out the word *fo-nay* you will find it means the tone of His voice, the disclosure of His voice. In other words, when you recognize His voice you recognize the tone and know that He is God. You are hearing God, not just any voice but His voice.

Do you recognize the voice of family members on the telephone without them telling you who they are? You can because of association. You have heard their voice enough times that you recognize it. You cannot recognize unless you have built a relationship. We discern the voice of God by hearing it so often. We discern the voice of God because we have been in His presence a lot, because we have read His Word and it has come alive to us. We begin to recognize His voice, the kind of things He says, the way He says them and the Spirit that is behind what He is speaking. It is the same way we recognize our loved ones when they call us on the telephone and do not give us their name.

Yet once more I shake not the earth only, but also heaven. This is speaking about the time that the Lord came down on Mount Sinai after the children of Israel had journeyed out of Egypt and had come to the Mount. God began to speak and everyone could hear it. It shook the earth.

God is saying, *"I am getting ready to talk louder, the way I did once before. I spoke to everyone, not just my prophets."*

When God had spoken before, He spoke from the top of the mountain and everyone heard it. The people went to Moses and asked him not to let God do that anymore. *"It scares us. It shakes us to the core. If He keeps talking, we might actually have to live right. We might have to quit sinning. We might actually have a relationship and dedicate ourselves. We don't want that Moses. You go up on the mountain and talk to God. Then come down and tell us."* This was the beginning of the prophets. From that time on the voice of God was silent to the regular person. God began to speak only to the prophets, priests and kings.

Hebrews 12:26 is a prophecy that is coming. We are going to begin to hear God at a new level, a louder level. Understand that you are going to have to be like the children of Israel and repent of some stuff because it is going to shake you. That voice is going to shake everything that is going to be shaken.

Yet once more I shake not the earth only, but also heaven. This heaven is where the principalities are.

Hebrews 12:27; *"And this word, Yet once more, signifieth the removing of those things that are shaken, as of things that are made, that those things which cannot be shaken may remain."*

In other words, His voice is going to shake stuff up. When He starts turning up the volume on His speaking, speaking louder and more distinctly people are going to have to recognize and deal with what He is saying. It is going to shake some people up, shake some nations up.

The only things that will not be shaken are those things that are dedicated and consecrated to Him. A good way to keep from getting shook loose is to make sure you have released your entire being unto God and belong to Him completely – spirit, soul and body.

The Bible speaks about a great falling away. There will be two aspects to this falling away. There will be a great incoming and a great exiting. People who are religious and playing games won't be able to handle it. They will be shook out of the picture.

Those who are hungry, not religious, but never had a chance will begin to hear and see. They will begin to come in. There will be a great influx of people coming into the kingdom of God.
At the same time, the religious bunch will find themselves on the outside. It is time to get real. Religion isn't going to cut it anymore. Having a form of godliness but denying the power thereof, the Bible says

from such to turn away.⁶ God is about to turn the power up on His speaking. He is raising up prophets everywhere in order for us to get prepared. He is getting ready to talk louder. He is getting ready to talk more. We had better be prepared for His voice.

Anytime God is getting ready to do something He sends those to go ahead and prepare the way. Before Jesus came, He sent John the Baptist to make the crooked places straight, to preach repentance. Repentance means coming back to God, turning the hearts of the people back to God, away from religion, away from man's way of reaching God. Religion is man's attempt to be holy, to make themselves feel like they are okay with God. It will not satisfy the Lord Jesus Christ. He doesn't want religion. He wants you to come, humbly bow before Him and allow Him to make you worthy. Allow Him to make you righteous. Allow Him to reach your heart.

Salvation is God touching man. Religion is man trying to reach God. The tower of Babel was man trying to reach God with his own efforts. So, God stopped it. He was not behind that. He knew it was the wrong spirit so He allowed confusion to get into it.

Salvation comes when we realize that without Him we are nothing. We can't do a thing without Him therefore we are going to hide ourselves in the rock. We are going to hide ourselves in Jesus. No matter what storm comes, we are hidden in Him. For you are dead, Paul said in Colossians, and your life is hid with Christ in God.⁷

Notice the rest of what Paul says here.

Hebrews 12:28-29; *"Wherefore we receiving a kingdom which cannot be moved, let us have grace, whereby we may serve God acceptably with reverence and godly fear: For our God is a consuming fire."*

---

⁶ 2 Timothy 3:5
⁷ Colossians 3:3

Paul is connecting God's fire with His voice. I guarantee that if you hear His voice very much, His fire will get on you and in you. Whenever He speaks, He is a consuming fire. His voice will consume you.

When you hear and accept His voice, the fire gets on you. It gets on you before it gets in you. Once it gets in you it will come out of you. When it comes out of you it is prophetic fire.

REFINING FIRE

Malachi 3:1; *"Behold, I will send my messenger, and he shall prepare the way before me:"*
This is speaking about John the Baptist. The Hebrew word for *"messenger"* is *mal-awk'*. It means the prophet. The prophets are going before to prepare the way for what God is about to do. That is why God is raising up prophets and prophetic people everywhere. There is an increase of the prophetic to prepare the way for what He is about to do.

Malachi 3:1-3; *"Behold, I will send my messenger, and he shall prepare the way before me: and the Lord, whom ye seek, shall suddenly come to his temple, even the messenger of the covenant, whom ye delight in: behold, he shall come, saith the LORD of hosts. But who may abide the day of his coming? and who shall stand when he appeareth? for he is like a refiner's fire, and like fullers' soap: And he shall sit as a refiner and purifier of silver: and he shall purify the sons of Levi* [the ministry]*, and purge them as gold and silver, that they may offer unto the LORD an offering in righteousness."*

The prophets are going ahead to prepare the hearts so that the Lord may release His refining fire. The refining fire is first going to come upon the ministry. Why?

Ministers cannot minister to the people unless they have first ministered to the Lord and God won't accept your ministry if there are things that have not been refined. That is why many ministries have no fire to give the people. They haven't received any fire because the Lord didn't accept what they brought to Him. Their prayer, their praise, what they were trying to do was their own thing. It wasn't what God wanted. God never sends fire down to consume a sacrifice that He doesn't accept and doesn't want.

The ministry is supposed to be releasing fire to the people, but they have to first get it. The Lord told me a long time ago that my first ministry was to Him. If I would minister to Him then He would give me the power to minister to others. If I don't minister adequately to Him, I don't get the adequate anointing and glory to release to others. It is the same principle. You can't release fire on other people if you have not acquired the fire yourself. You can't give what you do not have.

You don't have it if it is not a situation where you are purged to handle it so you have to let fire pure you. When it purges you then you become a pure metal in the eyes of God. You become a vessel of silver and gold, a vessel of honor and purity that fire can continue to flow through.

Another word for fire is lightening or electricity. There is electricity in lightening. There is no electrical movement of God, no real power that is electrical enough to change a life unless those metals of silver and gold (the ministry) are purged by fire.

When you have presented yourself to the Lord and you are willing for Him to refine you, He will. Until you are willing, though, you will never be refined with fire. A lot of the refining will come by Him talking to you. When He starts talking to you, pointing things out in your heart and your life those words burn and refine. Have you ever had the Holy Spirit speak to you and deal with you about things that needed to change and come out of you? I have been laid out in the Spirit, on the floor somewhere and all of a sudden God is dealing with me about some attitudes about things, things that needed to go. When I got up from there, I was different. He spoke and refined me so He could use me greater. Allow Him to do it. It will hurt for the moment but when you come out of it you have something to give somebody else.

LIFE CHANGING

This fire is life changing.

Acts 2:1; *"And when the day of Pentecost was fully come, they were all with one accord in one place."*

It was the day of Pentecost. The feast of Pentecost had begun.

Acts 2:2-3; *"And suddenly there came a sound from heaven as of a rushing mighty wind, and it filled all the house where they were sitting. And there appeared unto them cloven tongues like as of fire, and it sat upon each of them."*

The refining fire that came upon them was soon to be connected to speaking, to prophetic utterance. Are you aware that in 1 Corinthians 14 it says that tongues and interpretation is equal to prophecy? They are the same as prophecy. The interpretation is always the understanding, the revelation of what the message in tongues was.

Did you know that God has to purge our mouths? We are used to speaking our own words but you can't speak your own words and speak God's words. As long as you are speaking what you want to speak, you can't speak what He wants you to. It is a conflict of interest. Once the one thing is taken care of, you get the other and so our mouths have to be purged.

Isaiah told the Lord that he was not worthy to speak for Him. He was a man with unclean lips. In other words, he couldn't seek God's fire because there were things not right in him yet.[8]

When the fire comes, you may want to prophesy something bad to somebody and won't be able to. You will open your mouth and bless, bless, bless them when in your head you are thinking that they don't deserve that from God and you don't want to say it.

---
[8] Isaiah 6:5

The Word of God tells us in Isaiah 58:13 that we have to no longer speak our own words but we have to speak His words. If you want the full blessing of God to come upon you, you can no longer speak your words.

Isaiah 58:13-14; *"If thou turn away thy foot from the sabbath, from doing thy pleasure on my holy day; and call the sabbath a delight, the holy of the LORD, honourable; and shalt honour him, not doing thine own ways, nor finding thine own pleasure, nor speaking thine own words: Then shalt thou delight thyself in the LORD; and I will cause thee to ride upon the high places of the earth, and feed thee with the heritage of Jacob thy father: for the mouth of the LORD hath spoken it."*

There are some powerful things in this passage. The fact is that we need our mouth purged. We need that purging fire to purge our mouths and deliver us from ourselves so that we no longer walk around saying anything that comes into our head, saying a lot of negative things, saying what is opposite of the Word of God, speaking things to other people that are not what God wants us to say, speaking what we see instead of what He says. I have found out that when you prophesy you don't do it based on your own knowledge or what you feel or think about a situation. You have to be delivered from that. You need fire to purge your mouth.

Isaiah said, *"Lord, you are going to have to do something with me."* So, the Lord took a coal of fire from off the altar, touched his mouth and purged his words.[9]

Let's look at Leviticus 23 where Pentecost is talked about. By the way, this is the same Jewish feast we read about in Acts 2. We thought the word Pentecost meant tongues. It actually means fifty days. Fifty days after what? After Passover.

Leviticus 23:15-16; *"And ye shall count unto you from the morrow after the sabbath, from the day that ye brought the sheaf of the wave*

---

[9] Isaiah 6:6-7

offering; seven sabbaths shall be complete: Even unto the morrow after the seventh sabbath shall ye number fifty days; and ye shall offer a new meat offering unto the LORD."

Seven days times seven weeks equals forty-nine days. Add the day after and it is fifty days. This is Pentecost.

Leviticus 23:17; *"Ye shall bring out of your habitations two wave loaves of two tenth deals* [about a half gallon each of flour]*: they shall be of fine flour* [representing Jesus]*; they shall be baken with leaven* [leaven represents us]*; they are the firstfruits unto the LORD."*

They took the fine flour (representing Jesus), added water (representing the Holy Spirit), then added leaven to it (representing mankind), mixed it up and made two loaves (one representing the Jews, the other the Gentiles). Then they put the loaves in an oven. In these ovens, flames surrounded the bread to heat it. It is called baptizing the bread. They baptized two loaves of bread in fire until the leaven was baked out. There was no room for flesh anymore.

God cannot use us because we will spoil everything if the fire has not been applied to us and we are not baptized in fire. Have you ever seen people speak in tongues and live ungodly? I have seen them speak in tongues and then go around cutting Christians to pieces with their words. There is no fire there and God can't really use them in the prophetic.

SANCTIFYING FIRE

Luke 3:16; *"John answered, saying unto them all, I indeed baptize you with water; but one mightier than I cometh, the latchet of whose shoes I am not worthy to unloose: he shall baptize you with the Holy Ghost <u>and</u> with fire:"*

John G. Lake said he had gotten the baptism of tongues. Later on, he found out that he had not gotten the baptism of fire so he sought God for it. The baptism of fire is connected to tongues but it is different. He spoke in tongues a lot more but this time the fire was applied and it changed his personal life. After that, signs, wonders and miracles happened on a regular basis. God would give him a word and he would speak it. Signs and wonders would start happening. It was not hard. This is the baptism of fire.

We need a fire baptism going on until we not only get tongues but also we go into tongues of fire.

When you get baptized in fire, fire has to surround you. If fire surrounds you then that same fire that is purging you is also protecting you from the enemy.

Zechariah 2:5; *"For I, saith the LORD, will be unto her* [talking about His people] *a wall of fire round about, and will be the glory in the midst of her."*

He said He was going to be a wall of fire, a wall of protection. The Lord reminded me about the pillar of fire by night that kept the Egyptians from prematurely attacking the Israelites and destroying them before they had a chance to cross over the Red Sea to the other side.[10]

When you really enter the fire of God, it not only changes you but it releases a protective wall around you that satan cannot penetrate while he is trying to prematurely stop your vision, stop your call, stop your destiny, stop you from becoming what God wants you to be.

ZEAL AND DESIRE

Zeal and desire are the passion for God and the passion of God.

God gave me a revelation many years ago about His being pleased with obedience. Not with results but with obedience. The result is up to

---

[10] Exodus 14:24

Him. At the beginning of my ministry, the Lord would take me to little churches with just a handful of people. I would preach my heart out. Everyone there was saved, delivered, filled with the Holy Ghost and had miracles happen for them. I went through that kind of fire. After several of these kinds of churches I went before the Lord apologizing for being such a failure. He stopped me and asked me if I had done everything He had told me to do. I said, *"Yes, with all my heart."* He answered that then I was a success in His eyes. The pay and the reward in heaven is the same if you stand on a corner doing what He told you to do and see one person get saved or if you are ministering to thousands. All He is looking for is obedience. Function where He told you to function and He is happy with you.

God is looking for obedience, not natural man's success. From that time on, I am no longer looking for crowds but for whomever God sends me to. I have been to places where there were only one or two people and I poured my heart out. I gave them everything I had been fasting, praying and seeking God for. Both of them got healed, blessed and anointed. They shouted in joy at the presence of God. I was a success in God's eyes. And so are you if you are doing what He tells you to do.

Jeremiah, the prophet, had preached for a long time and had no converts. They wouldn't listen to him and he was ready to give up, to quit. Actually, he was making an impact because he was doing what God said but he didn't see it.

Jeremiah was ready to quit because he wasn't seeing natural success.

Jeremiah 20:9; *"Then I said, I will not make mention of him, nor speak any more in his name.* [He was not going to talk about God anymore.] **But his word** [His revelation, His rhema] *was in mine heart as a burning fire shut up in my bones, and I was weary with forbearing* [He could not quit. It was wearing him out trying not to speak.]*, and I could not stay."*

If you get a revelation of God's Word in your heart, it is hard not to say it to somebody. Whatever is big and alive on the inside of you is going to come out big and alive through your mouth. From the abundance of the heart, the mouth is going to speak.

Fire is simply a passionate desire or a zeal for God. Jesus said that the zeal of God had consumed Him.[11] Zeal is the fire of God burning within you. When you really have this fire on the inside of you, you can't get enough Word. You want to be in the anointing. You want to be where the Spirit of God is moving. You want to be where the Word of God is being preached and taught with power. You hunger and thirst after it. That is the zeal for God.

It is a sign that God is dealing in your life. If you don't have a passion for God that means there is an absence of God. Where His fire isn't, He isn't. Where His fire is, He is. Our God is a consuming fire. If you have fire inside of you it is a sign that God, the consuming fire, is in you. You have Him or you wouldn't have a fire. You can't have a desire for Him without Him.

You can tell when the saints are not revived and have no fire. They don't want to read their Bibles. They don't want to pray. They don't want to come to the house of God. Those are signs of the absence of the fire of God.

Revival is about getting an increase of fire in the hearts of people. When that happens, they can't stay away from church. They can't get enough Word. They can't do enough. They are hungry all the time for God.

When you keep nurturing and feeding the fire for God you will wind up getting the fire of God. The fire of God is God's desire to reach the nations. Have you ever noticed that when people get fired up for God and stay fired up they are going out along the highways and hedges, going to the nursing homes or the neighbors to tell somebody about Jesus. They are going into all the world to preach the gospel, starting at Jerusalem, Judea, Samaria, and going to the uttermost parts of the earth. If you keep

---

[11] Psalm 119:139

the fire for God burning you will get the fire and the zeal of God. The zeal of God is the nations.

GOD SPEAKS OUT OF THE FIRE

If you want Him to speak, get more fire. The more fire you have in you, the more He is going to talk to you and through you. He speaks out of fire. That means He is speaking out of zeal, out of burning desire for Him.

Deuteronomy 4:11-12; *"And ye came near and stood under the mountain; and the mountain burned with fire unto the midst of heaven, with darkness, clouds, and thick darkness. And the LORD spake unto you out of the midst of the fire: ye heard the voice of the words, but saw no similitude; only ye heard a voice."*

Similitude means a shape.

God spoke out of the burning bush. The fire that was burning got the attention of Moses, which is what fire is supposed to do. The fire of God will get our attention so that we start looking toward the fire, toward God. When we start to look toward the fire, we are about to hear God speak. If there is no fire, there will be no voice of God speaking. If there is no zeal for God, no zeal of God, no burning passion there will be no voice. If you want God to speak to you, to speak through you then you have to get the fire because He speaks out of the fire. If He is talking a little bit, you need to stoke the flames. You need more.

Deuteronomy 4:33; *"Did ever people hear the voice of God speaking out of the midst of the fire, as thou hast heard, and live?"*

Deuteronomy 4:36; *"Out of heaven he made thee to hear his voice, that he might instruct thee: and upon earth he shewed thee his great fire; and thou heardest his words out of the midst of the fire."*

Deuteronomy 5:4; *"The LORD talked with you face to face in the mount out of the midst of the fire,"*

Deuteronomy 5:22-25; *"These words the LORD spake unto all your assembly in the mount out of the midst of the fire, of the cloud, and of the thick darkness, with a great voice: and he added no more. And he wrote them in two tables of stone, and delivered them unto me. And it came to pass, when ye heard the voice out of the midst of the darkness, (for the mountain did burn with fire,) that ye came near unto me, even all the heads of your tribes, and your elders; And ye said, Behold, the LORD our God hath shewed us his glory and his greatness, and we have heard his voice out of the midst of the fire: we have seen this day that God doth talk with man, and he liveth. Now therefore why should we die? for this great fire will consume us: if we hear the voice of the LORD our God any more, then we shall die."*

We talked about this earlier. They were afraid the fire would consume them. It is supposed to even though they didn't want it to. God is a consuming fire. He wants to consume us with Himself until we are so consumed with God that everywhere we go all we want to do is talk about Him. He is talking to us and we are talking to Him. We are talking the revelation that He has given us. We are talking to Him about what He is talking to us about. That is being consumed with Him.

The Israelites were afraid God would consume them but that was what He wanted. They were afraid they would die. Yes, the part that would have died was the flesh. They wouldn't have actually died unless they hung on to their flesh.

Deuteronomy 5:26; *"For who is there of all flesh, that hath heard the voice of the living God speaking out of the midst of the fire, as we have, and lived?"*

The point is that they did live and they didn't like it.

Deuteronomy 5:27; *"Go thou near, and hear all that the LORD our God shall say: and speak thou unto us all that the LORD our God shall speak unto thee; and we will hear it, and do it."*

- Prophetic Fire & Glory -

Thank God for the prophets, however that is not God's best for us. He wants you to be dead to self so that you can hear Him out of the fire. God wants you to be consumed with Him so that He can speak to you out of that consuming fire that is within you.

My main job as an apostle and prophet is to equip the saints with the fire so they can hear God, so they can draw nigh to God and God can speak to them and through them. I have not done my job if I do all the hearing for the saints. That is not God's best. His sheep are supposed to hear His voice. As many as are led by the Spirit as the sons of God not as many as are led by the prophet.

Though I may prophesy to you to help release the prophetic into the air and release something prophetic in you, the prophetic is more than just me speaking something. Words carry things. Words are containers of good or bad. Because of my time with the Lord, when I speak to you, you will get more than words. What I have been filling up on is what will fill the words that I give to you. If I have been filling up with the fire, with His presence, with God then I have something to give you when I speak. We get more than words when we get a prophecy. What I want you to get is hearing ears. What I want you to get is a fire imparted. I want to impart such a desire for the spirit of God, for the supernatural of God within you that you cannot stand yourself anymore. You have to have it or die. Then you have had an impartation of fire.

We need prophetic fire. We cannot survive without it. How are we going to win this world without it? We can't.

When the fire began to set upon those in the upper room, they began to speak the wonderful works of God.[12] All the nations heard the prophecies through another tongue. They understood them and it was prophetic words to them and to their nations. Five thousand people turned to the Lord because of prophetic fire.

---

[12] Acts 2:11

Do you want to see people saved? Do you want to have an impact when you tell someone about Jesus? You won't if you have no fire. Fire will convince them. Fire will let them know that God is alive. Fire will tell them that He is Lord. Fire will let them know they need a savior.

Words that are not filled with fire are empty words that have little impact. Your words must be filled with desire fire, burning fire, compassion fire, passion fire, zeal fire so that when you speak them you are imparting. You are a prophetic fire starter and you are igniting hearts with a fire for God in order to have the fire of God.

How to Enter the Fire & the Glory

Philippians 4:15-19; *"Now ye Philippians know also, that in the beginning of the gospel, when I departed from Macedonia, no church communicated with me as concerning giving and receiving, but ye only. For even in Thessalonica ye sent once and again unto my necessity. Not because I desire a gift: but I desire fruit that may abound to your account. But I have all, and abound: I am full, having received of Epaphroditus the things which were sent from you, an odour of a sweet smell, a sacrifice acceptable, wellpleasing to God. But my God shall supply all your need according to his riches in glory by Christ Jesus."*

We want to pull out verse 19 and quote that when we have not given a sacrifice or have given one that does not smell good. Giving half of what God tells you to give won't smell good. Disobedience smells very bad and God will not send the fire down.

Today, the altar where the fire is sent is our hearts. When He sends the fire to our hearts there are the four manifestations we spoke about in the previous chapter.

Do you really want to be where God will trust you and release what He considers the treasure? That treasure is not always finances. Man considers natural things as treasure. God considers something else as being the treasure.

Luke 16:10-11; *"He that is faithful in that which is least is faithful also in much: and he that is unjust in the least is unjust also in much. If* *therefore ye have not been faithful in the unrighteous mammon, who will commit to your trust the true riches?"*

God calls money a least thing. We call it a big thing. We have to switch our thinking and think the way He thinks. We have to call money little and God's stuff big. The only way you can do it is to treat it that way. If you don't care about money you can give it away as quickly as you can get it and you prove to God that His stuff means more than your stuff. Only when His stuff means more than your stuff will you get His stuff. That is why many Christians are not using the deeper things of God on a regular basis.

Jesus also says in this verse that if you are unjust in your giving He can't trust you to promote you. He can't trust you with His power or with His anointing. He can't trust you with His glory. He can't trust you with ministries that are stronger and bigger than you. He can't trust you with the big because He can't trust you with the little. If He can't trust you with money, He can't trust you with power because you will corrupt it. God will test you with finances.

All the ministries I know that flow in creative miracles, in an awesome anointing are the most generous people I have ever seen. It looks like they give away more than they get. The Lord has connected me under these kinds of ministries. We have to become selfless instead of selfish if we want God to use us.

Being faithful with unrighteous mammon means you have been faithful in giving tithes and offerings.

If therefore ye have not been faithful in the unrighteous mammon, who will commit to your trust the true riches? This question has an implied answer. Nobody would trust you, including God. If God can trust you with finances and to do everything He tells you to do with them, not being afraid to obey when He tells you to do something then He will release to you the true riches of heaven – the anointings, the glory, the manifestations of creative power, the flow of everything He has. He will release ministries to you, opportunities to you if He can trust you. If He can't trust you then you won't get it. You may taste a little of it in order for God to give you a desire for it. You may say, *"Well, God has used me like that before."* My question to you is, *"Is He now?"* The reason He used you a little bit was to try and make you hungry enough for it that you would be willing to lay down anything.

People who flow on an ongoing basis in creative miracles are the people we are talking about. These are the people who have laid it down and said, *"God, whatever you want, whenever you want. My tithe is yours. My offerings are yours. Whatever you want whenever you want it, it is yours. I trust you. All if have to know is that this is what you are telling me. As soon as you tell me it is done."* Then the Lord will say, *"Okay, you are one I can trust with true riches. You are one I can trust to have it on an ongoing basis and to release it. I am going to give it to you."*

Think about employers. They start easing their people into more responsibility. If they can handle a little more then a little more will be given to them.

God wants to send the fire and the glory. He wants to show His face, reveal His true riches. Along the way we have to be giving ourselves to the Lord. We have to be willing to make covenant with God. If you want the true fire and glory in your life, every day of your life make a covenant with God that you belong to God. All that you have and all that you are, all that you will ever be is His. Anytime He says, *"This is what I want."* You say, *"Yes, Lord."* He may wake you up in the night and tell you He wants you to pray until the sun comes up. You will say okay and do it even though you are tired and your body doesn't want to. The Holy Ghost may tell you that He wants you to talk to a neighbor or bake something for someone. You say okay even though you have fifteen things already planned for your day. You just heard the covenant God talk to you and put a demand on you. You respond, *"Yes, sir, I will do it."* As soon as you do, you open the door for you to put a demand on God.

Many have been in our meetings where God started filling people's teeth with gold, silver and enamel. I did not lay hands on them, God did it. He was honoring covenant with me because I honored covenant with Him.

My wife and I had made a covenant vow to a ministry that was being used in the filling of teeth as well as other creative miracles. We had paid about a third of the vow. (Did you know that you could make payments on a vow? As long as you are paying on it, you are activating it.) The Holy Ghost spoke to my wife and she wrote a check for the balance. It cleaned out our account and we still had bills due.

I didn't know about her doing that. When I found out, my natural head started giving me a hard time, however my wife was hearing the voice of God. The Holy Ghost spoke to me and said, *"Are you going to let her be the only one to get the benefit out of this?"* I answered, *"No, Lord. I am going to get this thing straight right now. I am excited that she did it."* I wanted the vow to be paid though I don't know if I agreed on the timing. However, it was God's timing. I thank God for a wife who hears the Lord. She will obey God before she obeys me. Why, because there is a higher voice than mine. Her first husband is Jesus.

Before we got married, we told each other, *"You are not my first love."* Jesus is our first love. We also told one other, *"If you ever back out of Jesus I am going on without you."* We have to love Him more than we love people, even our mates.

So, I got my heart right on the payment of the vow and then I remembered covenant. *"Okay, Lord. You wanted us to do this. You asked us to do this. We cleaned out our account for this. I am not worried about the money because you always take care of us. If you tell us to do something you will bring the money in to pay the bills. You called covenant on my wife and me. We did what you said. Now, I am going to call covenant on you. In the next revival I have, I want you to start filling people's teeth with gold, silver and enamel, do creative miracles and remove tumors and growths without me laying hands on them."*

As soon as I said that, I went into a vision and saw God doing that. I also saw what I needed to do to help people receive it. It happened that fast.

At the next revival I got up and told the people what Jesus had said. He wanted to be their everything – their doctor, their lawyer, their banker, their savior, their deliverer, their dentist, their eye doctor. He said to me, *"Anything that my people will let me be for them, I will be that to them. I am all of these things but they have to allow me to do it. Have them begin to worship, look unto me, receive from me. I am the living bread. Receive everything I am, worship me, focus on me, and receive me as everything. Then tell them at the right moment to open their mouth because I will fill it."*

I began to flow with that in the service. We started with the breaking of bread and the people thinking of Jesus as the bread of life and began to worship the Lord, focusing on Jesus. We had a time of worship and waiting on God. Then the Lord had me to give them a scripture.

Psalms 81:10; *"I am the LORD thy God, which brought thee out of the land of Egypt: open thy mouth wide, and I will fill it."*

I told the people to open their mouth and the Lord would fill it. I told them it would look stupid but they were to sit there with their mouth open and love Jesus. The music kept playing. In a little bit the Lord let me feel what He was doing. I started feeling numbness in my jaw and started tasting copper. I also felt heat. I began telling the people what I was experiencing. The Lord told me there were some molars being filled, cavities being filled and I passed that on to the people. I told them that others were feeling heat. People started grabbing their jaws. Then I said if they were sensing something to come to the side of the room. One man said that all his fillings had fallen out and he had craters in his mouth. I told him to open his mouth. When he did I saw a flash of gold. All of those craters were filled with gold fillings.

Since that time, we have seen this happen to hundreds of people as they sat in the services. All of this has been happening because of the covenant relationship I have with God. He requires things from me and I can then turn around and require something from Him. Covenant will cause you to enter the fire and the glory. You cannot do it without covenant. Covenant will cost you everything but it will also get you everything.

Job 22:27; *"Thou shalt make thy prayer unto him, and he shall hear thee, and thou shalt pay thy vows."*

A vow is a promise to do something, to give something.

Job 22:28; *"Thou shalt also decree a thing, and it shall be established unto thee: and the light shall shine upon thy ways."*

Can you see that if while I am praying I make a vow and pay that thing, then I have the power to decree? I did that. I called God into covenant with me. Some would say that I don't have the right to do that but I do. I know of people, in the Word, who were in covenant and God caused the sun to stand still.[13] I have another one for you. Because of covenant God turned the sun back ten degrees.[14] Our covenant does make a difference with God.

the light shall shine upon thy ways The light is always connected to glory.

Isaiah 60:1; *"Arise, shine; for thy light is come, and the glory of the LORD is risen upon thee."*

The Lord spoke to me one time and said that there are spiritual side effects to our obedience in giving. A minister we are in covenant with told me if I were obedient in giving at all times that every time God would release something spiritual into me while I was releasing something natural to Him. There is always a transfer.

Righteousness is not money. It is right standing with God. Righteousness is not prosperity though prosperity is righteousness. Prosperity is a benefit of righteousness.

---

[13] Joshua 10:12-14
[14] 2 Kings 20:9-11

2 Corinthians 9:10; *"Now he that ministereth seed to the sower both minister bread for your food, and multiply your seed sown, and* [Paul had mentioned the natural and now tells about something spiritual that affects our harvest] *increase the fruits of your righteousness;"*

My obedience in giving increases the fruits of righteousness. What is the fruit of an intimate relationship with God? Righteousness is standing next to God, an intimate relationship with God.

Could the fruit be that I hear Him better, that I start being used by Him more, more power with God, more glory, more anointing? Could that be the fruit of righteousness? I believe so. It is tied to your giving.

Sow Prayer / Reap Fire

Revelation 8:1-5; *"And when he had opened the seventh seal, there was silence in heaven about the space of half an hour. And I saw the seven angels which stood before God; and to them were given seven trumpets. And another angel came and stood at the altar, having a golden censer; and there was given unto him much incense, that he should offer it with the <u>prayers of all saints</u> upon the golden altar which was before the throne. And the smoke of the incense, which came with the <u>prayers of the saints</u>, ascended up before God out of the angel's hand. And the angel took the censer, and filled it with fire of the altar, and cast it into the earth: and there were voices, and thunderings, and lightnings, and an earthquake."*

The prayers of the saints went up. An angel mixed incense with them and allowed them to go before the altar of God, which is the throne. Then after the prayers ascended before the Father to the altar, God released fire from the altar into the censer that the angel held. The angel cast the censer, filled with fire, to the earth. When he did, four things happened. Four manifestations came out of the fire that was cast to the earth: voices, thunderings, lightnings, and an earthquake. We will get into those and learn what they mean.

But first, I want to get into the two times it mentions the prayers of the saints. Prayers (plural) not just ***the prayer*** of the saints but ***prayers*** of the saints meaning that there should be a lot of prayer going on. It is also important for us to know that there are different types of prayer.

I am going to teach some about prayer before I teach on the four manifestations because if our prayers don't ascent, the fire won't descend. There are three basic types of prayer that should be operative in the body of Christ at all times. If any one of these three types of prayer is missing, the fire won't descend from heaven. It takes all three for the church to be on fire.

DEVOTIONAL PRAYER

Mark 1:35; *"And in the morning, rising up a great while before day, he went out, and departed into a solitary place, and there prayed."*

Jesus was a man of prayer and had His own prayer time. We see from Luke 6:12 that He prayed all night long. This prayer enabled Him to call forth the right men for disciples.

Praying all night long was part of His devotional prayer. Jesus prayed a great deal devotionally just to talk to His Father, to get connected with His Father.

The first thing we are going to have to instill in our lives is daily prayer. If you don't make prayer a priority, you will find out that you will seldom pray as you should. If you don't put it first, it will wind up last.

There are three parts of devotional prayer. First, you must set a time for prayer. If you don't set a time you won't pray. Satan will steal it from you. You'll say, *"I am going to pray sometime."* But then you get busy. This comes up and that comes up. Before long the whole day has gone by, you are asleep in bed and you didn't pray. So, you must have a prayer time. Jesus did.

You must have a prayer place, a place where you go to be alone to pray. It might be early in the morning in your living room. It might be in your bedroom. You must have a time and a place and you are the one to set it. If you build an altar of prayer to the Lord, He will come. Check out the life of Abraham. He built the altars. God will not build your altar for you. He will just show up after you build it. You must construct a prayer life. You have to build a better prayer life.

If you want a better prayer life, then start constructing it. Set a time and hold to it. Set a place and hold to it. I have found out that if you have a regular place to pray, you will sanctify that place and you will go back to that place more often.

Always have a purpose for prayer. It should not be petition. That is one type of prayer but if that is your focus then it won't draw you back to prayer. Relationship will. Focus your prayer life and make your purpose relationship, to be in His presence, to take the Word of God into it and read little segments of the Word in this prayer life, pray in the Holy Ghost, worship and love. If you ever get into the presence of God in your prayer life, it will draw you back every time. You have to press in.

There may be times when your prayer life seems dry. That is because you are digging a well. Every time you dig a new well it is hard, dry, dirty and takes a while. If you keep on digging, you will hit water. You always have to dig a new well when you go to a new level. If your prayer life is hard right now, rejoice because you have gone to a new level.

Dig the well. Give it a few weeks. It might be hard, dirty, and dry. Press on in. You may be praying in tongues and not feel a thing. You may be reading the Word and not thinking you are getting something out of it but you are. You are shoveling dirt. You will eventually hit water. Keep going.

Devotional prayer has to be built and has to be a daily thing. *"Daily will I seek thee."* You need fresh manna every day but you have to go and collect it. That means daily you have to get up and go collect the manna from God. You have to press in and do it. If you don't press in and do it, it won't be done. Nobody else can do your praying for you. Others can pray for you but they can't do your praying. They can pray with you but they cannot do your praying. Too many times we want ministry to do our praying. If more of God's children did their own praying, the less the ministry would have to pray so hard for you.

If you are always praying, you will always be receiving. You will eventually be tapping into some fresh water, getting some fresh manna and your life will change. God will hear your prayers and you will see some stuff going on. You could then go and help somebody else instead of always being so dependent and draining ministry.

It is time to grow up. Babies have to be feed and have everything done for them. As you grow up though, you can eventually go to the refrigerator for yourself.

CORPORATE PRAYER

Peter and John had been arrested and told they were not to preach Jesus Christ anymore. Instead of doing that, they went and got into a prayer meeting.

Acts 4:29-31; *"And now, Lord, behold their threatenings: and grant unto thy servants, that with all boldness they may speak thy word, By stretching forth thine hand to heal; and that signs and wonders may be done by the name of thy holy child Jesus. And when they had prayed, the place was shaken where they were assembled together; and they were all filled with the Holy Ghost, and they spake the word of God with boldness."*

Can you see that there is power in corporate prayer? We know from the Word that one can chase a thousand and two ten thousand.[15]

There is a mistake the body of Christ has been making because of some erroneous teaching. People have been teaching that one Christian can take care of the devil and all of the demons. That is not in the Word of God. One can chase a thousand. It doesn't say one can chase all of them. It is going to take the body of Christ to defeat satan, to take satan's entire kingdom down. It is dangerous for one child of God to rise up by

---

[15] Deuteronomy 32:30

themselves and think, "*I am going to take a principality over this area all by myself.*" They will fight some stuff they don't know how to handle. They will feel oppression because all of that will come down on their head. But add your prayers to another child of God and begin to come together.

Binding and loosing doesn't work very well unless there are two or three. It is time to realize that we are a body, not individuals. We are a body made up of individuals but we are to be linked to one another. I cannot make it without you. You can't make it without me. We need one another. We should be adding faith to faith, anointing to anointing, prayer to prayer, authority to authority. If we come together, we can take every stronghold down. By ourselves we can only chase a thousand.

I had to learn this the hard way. I had some stuff happen in my life, some stuff hit me that I could not handle and I wondered why. I went to God about it. God told me, "*You are not following My Word. You have been trying to take strongholds down by yourself and you had hit a battle you couldn't handle.*"

There is a story Jesus tells in the Gospel about a king not going into battle until he is sure he has sufficient to finish that thing.[16] That means enough fire power, enough people to overpower the enemy. Don't rise up to take on the devil all by yourself. Jesus is enough to handle him. The body of Christ corporately is enough to handle him but you by yourself can't.

This has not been taught and it is why there are Christians stopping their relationship with God. They are getting cold and quitting. Attacks come and marriages fail, finances fail, children become addicts and everything falls apart. Why? Because satan had twisted some theology and people are not studying their Bibles enough to realize that we are a body. As a body we can take the devil out. As a body we can overcome every struggle. By ourselves we are limited. It is the body of Christ that is supposed to come together as one man, Paul said in Ephesians 4.

---

[16] Luke 14:31

God told Gideon, "*I am going to cause you to take the enemy down as one man.*"[17] Then God gave him three hundred people. God had him stand up and have everyone to say and do the same thing. The sword of the Lord and of Gideon. The three hundred became as one and they took the Midianites down. I think it is time to come back to the Holy Scriptures and realize that I need you and you need me.

Together we can do it. Together the devil doesn't have a chance. Together we stand, divided we fall. If we are ever going to come to the place where our brothers and sisters are not constantly coming against an attack they can't handle and their lives fall apart, we need the wisdom of corporate.

That is why we need covering, why we need connections, why we cannot do this by ourselves. Every pastor needs a pastor. Every apostle needs an apostle. Every one of us needs each other. We need a link with one another. We need to love one another. Forget the jealousies, one being big and one being little. We are all needed in the body of Christ.

We cannot feel an independent spirit that says we don't need anybody else. That is not the Spirit of Christ. Jesus didn't even feel that way. He tried to get three disciples to pray for Him while He was in the garden. He kept coming back to them and asking them if they couldn't at least pray for one hour.[18] If Jesus the Son of God needed the prayers of others, needed the corporate how much more do you and I need the corporate?

PRAYER OF AGREEMENT

Matthew 18:18; *"Verily I say unto you, Whatsoever ye shall bind on earth shall be bound in heaven: and whatsoever ye shall loose on earth shall be loosed in heaven."*

---

[17] Judges 7:1-25
[18] Matthew 6:26-46

Binding and loosing. We all believe in it but when is it most effective?

Matthew 18:19-20; *"Again I say unto you, That if two of you shall <u>agree</u> on earth as touching any thing that they shall ask, it shall be done for them of my Father which is in heaven. For where two or three are <u>gathered together</u> in my name, there am I in the midst of them."*

The Greek word for *"agree"* is *soom-fo-neh'-o*. The first part *soom* means together. *Fo-neh'-o* means to sound. So *soom-fo-neh'-o* means to speak together, to pray together about the same thing, to agree. Can you see that the binding and loosing is most effective when two or three come together? If one can chase a thousand and two chase ten thousand then how many can three chase?

You can see already that binding and loosing is more effective with numbers. We increase our authority level ten times when there is another brother and sister praying with us. You increase your prayer power tenfold when there is at least another person praying with you and you are praying about the same thing. You are *soom-fo-neh-o*, sounding together, praying together about the same thing.[19] Ten times the power with every other person.

Remember, we read in Revelation 8 that the prayers of the saints ascend up.

Revelation 8:3-5; *"And another angel came and stood at the altar, having a golden censer; and there was given unto him much incense, that he should offer it with the prayers of all saints* [plural, not individual but corporate] *upon the golden altar which was before the throne. And the smoke of the incense, which came with the <u>prayers of the saints</u>, ascended up before God out of the angel's hand. And the angel took the*

---

[19] <u>Symphony Glory</u>, written by Phil Rich, teaches about the importance of learning to connect with each other and function as part of the body. When we come together in concert, in symphony, we add faith to faith, glory to glory, and anointing to anointing.

censer, and filled it with fire of the altar, and cast it into the earth: and there were voices, and thunderings, and lightnings, and an earthquake."

When the saints get these three forms of prayer going all the time then it is releasing these prayers upward to heaven. An angel will add incense to the prayers and let them float up to the Father. At that point the Father instructs the angel to release fire back to the earth. The fire came from the altar before the throne, God's fire. Voices, thunderings, lightnings and an earthquake come with the release of the fire.

VOICES

The first of the manifestations is voices.

Acts 13:26-27; *"Men and brethren, children of the stock of Abraham, and whosoever among you feareth God, to you is the word of this salvation sent. For they that dwell at Jerusalem, and their rulers, because they knew him not, nor yet the <u>voices of the prophets</u> which are read every sabbath day, they have fulfilled them in condemning him."*

The voices are the prophetic. With the fire comes an increase of the prophetic. If we are praying corporately, are praying devotionally, are praying in agreement God is sending down fire. One manifestation that comes out of fire is an increase of the prophetic flow of God in the earth. More prophets will be raised up than ever before. There will be more prophetic flow which means more people will see in the spirit, hear the voice of God and will experience God speaking and leading them.

THUNDERINGS

After the voices came the thunderings.

Psalms 29:1-3; *"Give unto the LORD, O ye mighty, give unto the LORD glory and strength. Give unto the LORD the glory due unto his* *name; worship the LORD in the beauty of holiness. The voice of the LORD is upon the waters: the God of glory thundereth: the LORD is upon many waters."*

The God of glory thundereth. It is the glory being talked about when this psalm talks about the thundering. It is talking about God's glory being manifested.

The Hebrew word for "*glory*" is *kawbode*. It means the weightiest thing about God. What makes Him God is His personality, His nature, His character, and His likeness. God is love. Without love, He wouldn't be God.

In Exodus 33, Moses went up on the mountain and asked the Lord to show him His glory. The Lord did not show him His mighty works and wonders. The first thing He said was that His goodness would pass before Moses. That sounds like His personality. The Lord would also reveal to Moses His name, which means His nature. God talked about His mercy and His attributes.

When we pray, as we should do so corporately, devotionally, in agreement and if it is going on all the time, then God's glory will thunder. We will see God's personality. His very person will be released in the earth. We will see Him manifest Himself.

There is a difference between the anointing and the glory. The anointing breaks yokes and looses people from burdens. It is the yoke destroying, burden removing power of God. The glory releases miraculous signs and wonders.

John 2:11; *"This beginning of miracles did Jesus in Cana of Galilee, and manifested forth his glory; and his disciples believed on him."*

Miracles that change water into wine are not anointing but glory. The anointing has a limitation. It will destroy yokes and lift burdens so that someone can be saved, get delivered and get healed. But anointing will never give you creative miracles nor will it give you signs and wonders. Only the glory can give you that. The raising of the dead is never done by an anointing.

John 11:4; *"Jesus saith unto her, Said I not unto thee, that, <u>if thou wouldest believe, thou shouldest see the glory of God</u>?"*

Then He raised Lazarus from the dead.

The Lord spoke to me and told me there was something greater than the anointing. I was wondering what it could be when He told me it was His glory. Anointing is His hand, His works. Glory is Him. Glory is His face. Glory is His presence. Glory is His person. That will do more for you than anything else.

If the church will pray corporately, devotionally and in agreement on a regular basis God says He will do some thundering. His glory will thunder in the earth. When His glory is seen He will draw all people to Himself.

I have prayed for people and seen all kinds of healings take place but it didn't seem to shake people. I have also been in places where I didn't do anything and all kinds of miracles took place. Teeth were filled, tumors disappeared, organs that were gone were replaced and it shook the area. I didn't even touch anyone. With the anointing I have to touch somebody. With the glory, He touches somebody. Which one is better?

I am not putting down the anointing. It is a gift and a wonderful thing. But it has limitations. If you are anointed there is a danger people will look to you and worship you instead of God. When the glory hits, there is no chance of people looking to you. God gets it all because you are not doing a thing. He is doing it.

If the church will pray, He will send some thundering.

LIGHTENINGS

Ezekiel 1:13-14; *"As for the likeness of the living creatures, their appearance was like burning coals of fire, and like the appearance of lamps: it went up and down among the living creatures; and the fire was bright, and out of the fire went forth lightning. And the living creatures ran and returned as the appearance of a flash of lightning."*

When we pray, as we should, God will also increase the release of angelic visitations. It comes with the fire.

A good example of that is the time when Peter was in prison about to get his head cut off. The church got together and started praying corporately.[20] In the night, God sent angels.

Prayers were going up. God sent fire down. In the midst of the fire are the angels. They come out of the fire that has been sent to the earth because of the prayers going up.

Angels are sent to assist us, to help us. They are fellow ministers. They are there to minister for us, the heirs of salvation.[21] God will send angels to do what we cannot do. Angels will never do what you can do. They won't do your praying. They won't pay your tithes for you. They won't do your witnessing for you. You have to do your part but they will do what you cannot.

---

[20] Acts 12:5-10
[21] Hebrews 1:14

EARTHQUAKES

There are going to be some earthquakes that will come out of the fire. We are talking about spiritual earthquakes that affect the natural for the good, not for evil.

Acts 16:25-26; *"And at midnight Paul and Silas prayed, and sang praises unto God: and the prisoners heard them. And suddenly there was a great earthquake, so that the foundations of the prison were shaken: and immediately all the doors were opened, and every one's bands were loosed."*

We always talk about Paul and Silas praising, but that is not the first thing they did. First they prayed. If you can't pray through, you have nothing to praise about. Sometimes you have to pray through and get the victory over the thing, get it settled with God and then start shouting. If you had been persecuted for preaching, beaten and put into stocks, maybe you would have to pray through too. They prayed, meaning they sent prayers upward.

What does the earthquake in this scripture represent? Deliverance, the deliverance ministry that sets the captives free. When the prayers go up, the fire comes down and deliverance flows.

CONCLUSION

We see that we sow prayer and reap fire. Out of the fire comes the prophetic voice of God and prophecy begins to increase. Out of the fire comes the glory of God, the thunderings. Out of the fire come the lightnings and angelic visitation is increased everywhere. Out of the fire come earthquakes, which is the deliverance ministry, all kinds and facets of it.

All of these manifestations simply mean that God is doing His stuff. God Himself has come down to walk among men. He is releasing the fullness of Himself in the earth. If we want God to come in and be God, if we want God to flow in the earth we have to be willing to pray, willing to sow to the heavens to reap His fire in the earth.

Exodus 19:3-6; *"And Moses went up unto God, and the LORD called* [here is the voice] *unto him out of the mountain, saying, Thus shalt thou say to the house of Jacob, and tell the children of Israel; Ye have seen what I did unto the Egyptians, and how I bare you on eagles' wings, and brought you unto myself. Now therefore, if ye will obey my voice indeed, and keep my covenant, then ye shall be a peculiar treasure unto me above all people: for all the earth is mine: And ye shall be unto me a kingdom of priests, and an holy nation. These are the words which thou shalt speak unto the children of Israel."*

Remember, the first manifestation was the voice. The Lord began to speak up on the mountain.

Exodus 19:16-18; *"And it came to pass on the third day in the morning, that there were thunders* [the second manifestation] *and lightnings* [the third manifestation]*, and a thick cloud upon the mount, and the voice of the trumpet exceeding loud; so that all the people that was in the camp trembled. And Moses brought forth the people out of the camp to meet with God; and they stood at the nether* [lower] *part of the mount. And mount Sinai was altogether on a smoke, because the LORD descended upon it in fire* [we talked about fire coming down]*: and the smoke thereof ascended as the smoke of a furnace, and the whole mount quaked* [the fourth manifestation] *greatly."*

We see that all four of the manifestations come out of the fire.

Hebrews 12:29; *"For our God is a consuming fire."*

Those four manifestations that come out of the fire are manifestations of God. They are God's personality, God speaking, God moving. We are limited but He isn't. We need God. There are things we can pray about, desire to do but if God doesn't show us and do something, we are all in trouble.

We have to get God into our problem, get God into the earth, and get God into the situation. How are we going to do it? We need to sow into the heavens the prayers of the saints with devotional prayer daily, corporate prayer as often as we can, and the prayer of agreement. We send prayer to the heavens and God sends down the fire. When the fire hits the earth, these four manifestations of the prophetic, of the glory, of angelic visitation, and of deliverance will be in abundance.

Romancing the Flame

Exodus 25:22; *"And there I will meet with thee, and I will commune with thee from <u>above</u> the mercy seat, from <u>between</u> the two cherubims which are <u>upon</u> the ark of the testimony, of all things which I will give thee in commandment unto the children of Israel."*

"*Meet*" is a very unique Hebrew word. It is more than just showing up and hanging out. *Yaw-ad* means an appointment, to gather together (literally) for the purpose of engagement and to be betrothed. God is talking about a romance going on. God doesn't want to hang out like friends would. He wants to get together with us and come into a relationship. He wants us to be married. He wants to meet with you, wants to be engaged to you.

God also want to commune with you. "*Commune*" is a Hebrew word (*daw-bar'*) that means to speak and to answer. The Greek counterpart to the Hebrew is *koinonia*. It means coming into intimacy with. God wants to come into relationship with you, be engaged to you and court you. He is interested in a love relationship, in intimacy with you. Then He tells us where He wants this to take place. We are going to look at these three places but not in the order the scripture gives.

First all of this engagement and courting will take place ***above the mercy seat***. "*Mercy seat*" (Hebrew: *kaw-far*) means to cover, to forgive, to cancel and to pardon. Mercy seat represents total pardon, total forgiveness, the cancellation of all the wrong that you and I have ever done. What God is saying is that for us to meet there has to be at the place of pardon. We have to meet at the place where all of our debts (spiritually) are cancelled, where all of our sins are pardoned, wiped out, disannulled as if we had never done them. Justification means *"just as if I'd never sinned."*

Isaiah 55:7; *"Let the wicked forsake his way, and the unrighteous man his thoughts: and let him return unto the LORD, and he will have mercy upon him; and to our God, for he will abundantly pardon."*

Whoever is the president or the top individual of authority has the ability to pardon. He can pardon whosoever he wishes, no matter what they have done. People can say what they want but he can do it because he has the authority level. Our Lord has the ultimate authority.

The word *"Lord"* (Greek: *koo'-ree-os*) means supreme authority. The supreme authority over a nation can pardon whomever no matter what. Saying something about it won't change it. Our God can look down on our lives and say, *"I pardon you."* You can say, *"Oh, God, I don't deserve it. I did some horrible things."* He still says, *"I pardon you."* And it is done, whether you feel it or not. Pardon is not based on feelings but on fact. It is in His Word, He has done it. The very word *mercy seat* means a place of pardon.

He wants to meet us above the mercy seat. Why above? He cannot meet us on the mercy seat because He is sitting there. When I tell my granddaughter to go to my rocker, she usually waits for me there. She does not want to sit in the chair but she wants in my arms. Above the mercy seat means in His arms. Are you beginning to see the romance that is going on? We are going to sit in His lap. We are going to commune with Him above the mercy seat not on the mercy seat.

Words are everything in the Bible. It didn't say He was going to commune with you *"on."* It said *"above"* it because that is where God is. God's presence sits on the mercy seat. Anything above it would be in His arms.

God is saying, *"I want to meet with you, get engaged, have an appointment of engagement with you. I want to enter a special koinonia relationship with you where you and I talk. You ask questions and I answer them. We will talk and commune with each other. The place it is going to happen is above the mercy seat where I can hug you, where I can hold you."*

The Lord wants a romance going on. The greatest love story every told is Jesus dying on the rugged cross to redeem us. We are called His bride and He is the groom. There is a marriage supper coming up which means there is a marriage going to take place. The consummation of it, the finalization of it will take place in the sky. Right now, though, God is saying He wants an engagement, a romance going on. God wants to court us. The place we will meet is right above the mercy seat. I hope you fall in love with Him as much as He is in love with you.

So first, He wants to meet us above the mercy seat. He also wants to meet us **upon the ark of the testimony**. *"Upon"* is talking about according to, because of, by reason of. Upon the ark of the testimony is upon the Word of God. *"I want this relationship to be according to the Word, because of the Word and by reason of the Word. I want the foundation of the relationship to be my Word."*

We are going to look at what was in the ark of the testimony. Testimony means witness.

Hebrews 9:4; *"Which had the golden censer, and the ark of the covenant overlaid round about with gold, wherein was the golden pot that had manna, and Aaron's rod that budded, and the tables of the covenant;"*

There were three things in the ark of the testimony. They all represent the Word of God but let's look at what they represent individually.

The pot full of manna represents the fact that they had to go out early in the morning every day and collect the manna. The manna represented a fresh Word from God. God's Word feeds us and provides sustenance for us. The golden pot represents us as vessels filled with this fresh Word that we got in our communing time with the Lord. As we were studying the Word and reading it we are getting manna, fresh revelation from it. With that we fill the pot, which is the vessel.

The pot represents fresh revelation that we get from digging into the Word of God daily. It is upon that foundation that this intimate relationship springs forth.

Numbers 17 tells the story of Aaron's rod that budded. It is an interesting story and I suggest that you read it. Basically what happened was that there was a lack of respect for the ministry. Some rose up and said, *"We can hear God just as good as the ministers can. We are just as anointed as anybody else."* Moses finally said, *"We are going to see if what you are saying is true. If the ground opens up and swallows you, we will know that you are not telling the truth."* It did just that. The ground opened up and swallowed the bunch that was saying they were just as anointed as Moses and Aaron.

Later there was still some controversy and so Moses said that the heads of the tribes should bring their rods. They were going to have a test to find out who was God's choice to bring forth leadership with the Word of God. Overnight, Aaron's rod budded, showing that he was the one called into full-time ministry.

We are all called into the ministry but don't ever lose respect for the five-fold ministry that God has placed over you. They will teach you and share the Word of God with you. Yes, you can study the Word for yourself and do all of that but understand there are different callings and different anointings. Abide in the calling where with you are called and never disrespect the callings and the anointings of the five-fold ministry. They are responsible for your soul, Hebrews tells us. They have to give an account. God will hold them responsible for you. Don't make it grievous for them but a joy. Though God can use you in a powerful way, there is a distinction when it comes to five-fold ministry because God has empowered them to train you in the Word of God.

Aaron's rod budding is respect for the ministry of the Word and the five-fold ministry who is going to train you in the Word.

This relationship has to be upon the revelation of the Word of God, the fresh manna that we get everyday and the respect for the five-fold ministry who is training us, helping us grow up until we look like Jesus and act like Jesus. Not a misfit for the Lord but an able bride. The five-fold ministry is equipping you to be that able bride for Jesus. They are going to help you with your love relationship with Jesus.

Now, let's look at the fact that all of this is going to take place **between the two cherubims**. He said it is going to happen above the mercy seat, between the cherubim and upon the ark of the testimony.

The tables of the covenant are the Word of God that is imparted and written by the Holy Ghost upon the tablets of our heart.[22] The Word of God is the basis for any relationship with Jesus Christ.

These are the three things that were within the ark of the testimony.

We are going to have some special times between the cherubim. We need to go back to Exodus 25 to see how the cherubim do not take credit to themselves. They are pointing toward what is between them.

Exodus 25:20; *"And the cherubims shall stretch forth their wings on high, covering the mercy seat with their wings, and their faces shall look one to another; toward the mercy seat shall the faces of the cherubims be."*

They are literally pointing their wings and faces toward the Lord who is between them.

Now, let's talk about the fire since the title of this chapter is "Romancing the Flame." The flame is Jesus.

Ezekiel 10:2; *"And he spake unto the man clothed with linen, and said, Go in between the wheels, even under the cherub, and fill thine hand*

---

[22] 2 Corinthians 3:3

with coals of fire from between the cherubims, and scatter them over the city. And he went in in my sight."

We are going to see that God dwells between the cherubim and that there are coals of fire between the cherubim.

Ezekiel 10:7; *"And one cherub stretched forth his hand from between the cherubims unto the fire that was between the cherubims, and took thereof, and put it into the hands of him that was clothed with linen: who took it, and went out."*

Remember the Lord said He was going to commune with us from between the wings of the cherubim.

The throne of God is also full of fire.

Daniel 7:9; *"I beheld till the thrones were cast down, and the Ancient of days did sit, whose garment was white as snow, and the hair of his head like the pure wool: his throne was like the fiery flame, and his wheels as burning fire."*

Psalms 80:1; *"Give ear, O Shepherd of Israel, thou that leadest Joseph like a flock; thou that dwellest between the cherubims, shine forth."*

Isaiah 6:6-7; *"Then flew one of the seraphims unto me, having a live coal in his hand, which he had taken with the tongs from off the altar: And he laid it upon my mouth, and said, Lo, this hath touched thy lips; and thine iniquity is taken away, and thy sin purged."*

The angel took the coal of fire, touch Isaiah's lips and his sin was purged. It actually was not a coal as much as it was a stone of fire.
We are seeing that the Lord is saying, *"I want to have this special relationship with you in the midst of my fire, my passion, my desire."* Fire means passion and desire when it comes to spiritual things. It also means zeal.

- Prophetic Fire & Glory -

Remember when Jesus went in and cleared the temple. He said, *"The zeal of my house has eaten me up."*[23] That word zeal means fiery passion.

There is passion, zeal, and extreme hot desire in fire. Once you start communing with the fire of God, start romancing the fire of God then that fire literally gets in you and on you and you start becoming passionate, zealous, and desirous of more of God. The end result of staying in that flame is that you not only pick up the passion for God but you also begin to pick up the passion of God, which is to win the world.

The Lord is saying, *"I want to be engaged to you. I want to romance you. The way I want this to happen above the mercy seat. That is where I pardoned you and you can get up in my arms because of that pardon. I want to hold you, love you. The foundation of all of this is my Word. We are going to be right between the cherubim, which means we will be right in the fiery passion of my love for you. We will be in the midst of the fiery passion of my desire for you, the fiery passion of my zeal for you until it is imparted inside of you. Then you will become not only passionate for me but also passionate for the world."* You become a fire starter wherever you go.

I have done some research on fire. The hottest flame is a blue flame. The hottest flame would be God. A natural blue flame averages 2,000° and above. Though fire has a consuming ability because it is very hot, it doesn't obliterate another substance as if that substance never existed. It changes the substance into another substance. There is a metamorphosis that takes place and it will never be the past substance again. It becomes a brand new substance that it never was before. With the hot flame, old things are passed away and all things have become new.

When you come in contact with the fire of God, the old man is gone. You are changed into a new man, a new substance with totally different properties.

---

[23] John 2:17

Natural things parallel the supernatural, spiritual things. Natural things help us understand supernatural things.

Hebrews 12:29; *"For our God is a consuming fire."*

He is going to consume what you used to be and then transform you into what you need to be. You don't have to worry about changing yourself. The blue flame will do it. Just draw close enough and let the flame touch you.

Once you are changed from the old substance to the new you can handle what the flame does. The structure of the new man cannot only handle the flame but it takes on the same properties of the flame. In other words, you become a flame.

Hebrews 1:7; *"And of the angels he saith, Who maketh his angels spirits, and <u>his ministers</u> [humans] <u>a flame of fire</u>."*

Do you know why the three Hebrew children could not burn in the fire? There is a reason why natural fire couldn't touch them. They were already burned up. You can't burn something twice. When it is burned it is burned. You can't change it anymore. They had already been burned by another fire that changed them to such a degree that the natural fie could not harm them.

Isaiah 43:2; *"When thou passest through the waters, I will be with thee; and through the rivers, they shall not overflow thee: <u>when thou walkest through the fire, thou shalt not be burned; neither shall the flame kindle upon thee</u>."*

But that is only if you have enough of the blue flame.

I believe it is possible to be so consumed with the blue flame that natural fire cannot light upon you. How do we know the three children had the blue flame? He was walking in there with them. The natural fire didn't burn Jesus because He is fire. It didn't burn them because they had Him, the fire.

Are you ready to start romancing the flame? This is a love relationship. We are drawing nigh unto Him. We are running to the flame, to Him. The Song of Solomon says, *"Call me and I will run. Draw me and I will run."*

The fire brings the glorification of God once you have come into the fire relationship. We come back to the fact that spiritual fire is passion for God. It starts out a passion for God and winds up the passion of God. You will get both of them eventually if you stay in it long enough. I can tell if someone has the passion for God because they will wind up with the passion of God and will want to win the world to Jesus Christ. Someone does not have much of the passion for God will not have the passion of God and not really care. You can't really care unless you are changed and you are not changed unless there is fire.

This love relationship is heart-to-heart, spirit-to-spirit. It is a direct connection with Jesus Christ. He is drawing us to Himself, calling us to Himself. He wants you more than you want Him. He wants to meet you and commune with you. He wants an engagement, a relationship.

He wants to court you. Why? Because He loves you. You want to be with somebody you love. You want to express your love. You want to be able to commune, open your heart and share whatever is in your heart. You want to be able to say something stupid and it be okay. You don't want to be made fun of. You want to open up and tell somebody how you feel, wrong or right this is what you are going through. It is safe. You are not going to be judged.

Jesus is just like that. There have been times I have opened my heart to Him and told Him how I feel about something, told Him what I am going through. If some other Christian had heard it, they would have judged me for it. But the Lord didn't. He is not religious. He knows when I am hurting. He knows how I feel. He does not condemn me for what I am feeling. Remember, He is meeting me at the mercy seat.

Our God is a loving, forgiving, pardoning God. He is not trying to find something so that He can excommunicate you. He just wants to love you, help you, be close to you, and be intimate with you. He likes you and loves you more than you like and love yourself. He thinks more of you that you think of yourself. He sees more potential in you than you see in yourself. Can you imagine someone looking at you and seeing the blueprint of why you were made instead of the mistakes you have made? Can you imagine someone who looks at you, sees the very reason you were born and sees the stuff in you that you are going to become?

He will never abuse you, use you and throw you aside. He will never see the faults in you and eject you out of His graces. The only way you are out and away from God is by your choice. If you don't want God, that is okay. He will cry over that but He will let you have your way.

No matter how many mistakes I make, as long as I say, *"Lord, I need you. I don't ever want to be without you."* Then I never will be. His grace, His love and His mercy is enough to cover me. The mercy seat also means the covering. I hope you can understand that you are loved by God and not condemned by Him. God is not looking for a loophole to get you on.

Satan is legalistic. He is looking for one little detail so he can pounce on you. God isn't.

The mercy seat is a place where everything is pardoned, where everything is cancelled, where everything is forgiven, where everything is covered. Right above that place where you know you are forgiven is the place where He wants to wrap His arms around you.

House of Fire / House of Glory

2 Chronicles 7:1-4; *"Now when Solomon had made an end of praying, the fire came down from heaven, <u>and consumed the burnt offering and the sacrifices</u>; and the glory of the LORD filled the house. And the priests could not enter into the house of the LORD, because the glory of the LORD had filled the LORD'S house. And when all the children of Israel saw how the fire came down, and the glory of the LORD upon the house, they bowed themselves with their faces to the ground upon the pavement, and worshipped, and praised the LORD, saying, For he is good; for his mercy endureth for ever. Then the king and all the people <u>offered sacrifices</u> before the LORD."*

Notice, they had just finished offering sacrifices, turned around and did it again. If something works, then work it. Experiments have been done where monkeys have been taught to push a button to get a food treat. After a while the monkeys will continue to push the button because they have learned what happens when they do. Sometimes monkeys are smarter than people. I have seen people give, God bless them big and they never give again.

2 Chronicles 7:5-12; *"And king Solomon offered a sacrifice of twenty and two thousand oxen, and an hundred and twenty thousand sheep: so the king and all the people dedicated the house of God. And the priests waited on their offices: the Levites also with instruments of musick of the LORD, which David the king had made to praise the LORD, because his mercy endureth for ever, when David praised by their ministry; and the priests sounded trumpets before them, and all Israel stood.*

Moreover Solomon hallowed the middle of the court that was before the house of the LORD: for there he offered burnt offerings, and the fat of the peace offerings, because the brasen altar which Solomon had made was not able to receive the burnt offerings, and the meat offerings, and the fat. [There was so much Solomon had to move the offerings to the middle of the house instead of using the brazen altar.] *Also at the same time Solomon kept the feast seven days, and all Israel with him, a very great congregation, from the entering in of Hamath unto the river of Egypt. And in the eighth day they made a solemn assembly: for they kept the dedication of the altar seven days, and the feast seven days. And on the three and twentieth day of the seventh month he sent the people away into their tents, glad and merry in heart for the goodness that the LORD had shewed unto David, and to Solomon, and to Israel his people. Thus Solomon finished the house of the LORD, and the king's house: and all that came into Solomon's heart to make in the house of the LORD, and in his own house, he prosperously effected. And the LORD appeared to Solomon by night, and said unto him, I have heard thy prayer, and have chosen this place to myself for an house of sacrifice."*

There are several things in this scripture we are going to look at.

A HOUSE OF PRAYER

First, in order to have a house of fire and glory there has to be a house of prayer. 2 Chronicles 6 contains the prayer that Solomon prayed in the house. Chapter 7, verse 1 begins *"Now when Solomon had made an end of praying."*

Not only is there a gathering that is called a house but we individually are also called the house of the Lord. Paul said, *"Know ye not that ye are the temple (house) of God, and that the Spirit of God dwells in you?"*[24] If we want fire and glory in the corporate house and in the individual house we must have a house of prayer.

---

[24] 1 Corinthians 3:16

Isaiah 56:7; *"Even them will I bring to my holy mountain, and make them joyful in my house of prayer"*

We like to think of the corporate house of God as a house of prayer but we must see that prayer has to be the number one thing on our personal agenda as well. We shared this in the chapter on "Sowing Prayer/Reaping Fire." If prayer is your number one thing, you will find that God will begin to move in a tremendous way on your behalf. You will see the fire of revival.

2 Chronicles 7:14; *"If my people, which are called by my name, shall humble themselves, and pray, and seek my face, and turn from their wicked ways; then will I hear from heaven, and will forgive their sin, and will heal their land."*

Prayer, coupled with the Word of God, should be the most important thing of your day. Your devotion time is the most important thing in your life. If you want to put God first, then put prayer first. The way you put God first is to put prayer first, which means you are putting Him first. You are praying to God.

Prayer is not just entreating. It is putting God first, being with God, visiting with God. When you visit with God you are fellowshipping with Him, spending time with Him and that means you are putting Him first.

The first commandment says, *"Thou shalt have no other gods before me."*[25] There is a way to know if there is a god in your life because your number one priority is your god. I am talking about the priority of time. The things we value as important will get the time in our day. Some worship the flesh and want to give the body some extra time to sleep. Others worship God, which means they put the flesh under. Some want to worship God but only when it is convenient. He is supposed to be a priority. We want the blessings of God, the fire of God, the fullness of God but we don't want to dedicate and make Him number one. He does not pour out His best on those who make Him number two or three. He

---

[25] Exodus 20:3

pours out His best on those who make Him number one. God will honor you because you are honoring Him.

If you will put God first, the rest of what you need to get done in your day will get done. You can't afford not to pray just like you can't afford not to pay your tithes. Those who can afford not to pray can afford failure. Failure is connected with prayerlessness. The divorce rate among couples that pray together is almost zero. The divorce rate among Christian couples that don't pray together is fifty-seven percent.

My prayer life is vitally important to me, to my relationships, to my marriage, to my children, to my home, for my finances, for blessings and for eternity. Make prayer priority one and you will be making God number one.

A HOUSE OF SACRIFICE

In 2 Chronicles 7:1, when Solomon had made an end of praying the fire came down and consumed the burnt offering and the sacrifices. God will not consume something that you don't offer to Him. Anytime God consumes something, there is always an exchange. Since God only has good gifts to give, guess what we come up with. We get good gifts in exchange. All good and perfect gifts come from above.[26] God always releases something better back into your hands.

Remember, sacrifice is not a sacrifice until it is a sacrifice. How do you know if you are offering a sacrifice? Was it a sacrifice to do it? Did it cost you something?

In 2 Samuel 24 there is a story of a plague that came because of some things David had done. He had numbered the people when he shouldn't have because God had told him not to. David's motive was wrong. He was looking to the arm of flesh instead of looking to the arm of God. God did not want him to look at his might to determine whether or not he could do it.

---

[26] James 1:17

But David looked to the arm of flesh, numbered the people and a plague was released. Over seventy thousand people died and the plague was headed to Jerusalem. That meant David's family would be threatened.

The prophet came to David and told him there was something he could do to stop it. David asked what and was told to offer sacrifice. So, he went to the threshing floor of Araunah and told him what he needed for the sacrifice. Araunah was just going to give it to David because he was the king but David stopped him and told him that he had to pay full price for everything. *"I can give nothing to God that cost me nothing."*

It has to cost in order for there to be a return. God won't give much in exchange for something that hasn't cost you anything.

David made sacrifice to the Lord. As soon as God saw it, He commanded the death angel to stop in his tracks right outside of Jerusalem.

I have heard people say that today we don't have sacrifices. Not so. I am going to show you three new covenant sacrifices that we have today.

The first one is called the living sacrifice. We are the living sacrifice.

Romans 12:1; *"I beseech you therefore, brethren, by the mercies of God, that ye present your bodies a living sacrifice, holy, acceptable unto God, which is your reasonable service* [or worship].*"*

Getting up in the morning and praying when you don't want to is being a living sacrifice. Giving in an offering when you don't want to is being a living sacrifice. Witnessing to your neighbor when you don't want to because you are scared is being a living sacrifice. Praying for someone when you don't really want to is being a living sacrifice.

Then there is a sacrifice of praise.

Hebrews 13:15; *"By him therefore let us offer the sacrifice of praise to God continually, that is, the fruit of our lips giving thanks to his name."*

We are to offer up sacrifices of praise continually. That means there will be times when I don't feel like praising God. There will be times when things are not going the way I want them to go, when someone does something to me or says something to me that upset me and I don't feel like praising God but I am going to offer a <u>sacrifice</u> of praise. *"God, I am going to praise you anyway. In the midst of what I am going though, I am going to praise you."*

I have found that the most beneficial time to pray is when it is the hardest to pray. Those are the times you need to pray the most. Those are the times you will see the greatest victory. You will see the greatest breakthrough in you life when you can praise God when you don't want to, when you can praise God when you don't feel like it, when you can praise God when your body is hurting, when you can praise God when your family is in an uproar, when you can praise God in the middle of everything that is happening – God doesn't change even though your circumstances are. When you get some bills in the mail that you didn't expect and they are more than you expected them to be that is a time to praise God. *"God, I praise you that you can handle this. You are more than enough. Praise God that I have you. Praise God that I don't have to handle this by myself. I thank you Lord that you are going to see me through in this situation."*

Want the fire to fall and consume something? Where is the sacrifice? Fire falls for s reason. The fire of God always falls because there is something to be consumed, because there is something offered up that God sees as being worthy to send fire for.

The third kind of sacrifice is called the sacrificial offering.

Philippians 4:18; *"But I have all, and abound: I am full, having received of Epaphroditus the things which were sent from you, an odour of a sweet smell, a sacrifice acceptable, wellpleasing to God."*

Paul is saying that God smelled of the sacrifice they had given and He liked what He smelled. God doesn't send the fire down to consume a sacrifice unless the sacrifice smells good to Him.

We have an altar today that is called our heart. That is the altar where you offer up sacrifice. Even though you may give in a basket, you first offered it on the altar of your heart, where God looked it over and smelled it. If it is what He desires, if it smells good like a sweet smelling savor of a sacrifice acceptable then He sends the fire to consume it. The fire will come upon the altar of your heart.

2 Chronicles 7:1; *"Now when Solomon had made an end of praying, the fire came down from heaven, and consumed the burnt offering and the sacrifices; and the glory of the LORD filled the house."*

Offerings and sacrifices can be the same thing but they can also be different. You can give an offering and it not be a sacrifice. Your sacrifice is definitely your offering. It is all included. Whenever you give an offering, you are giving something out of love. A sacrifice will cost you something.

We have the idea that today we only have offerings. We have sacrifices also. It is the sacrifice that causes the fire to fall. The three areas of sacrifice are: ourselves as a living sacrifice, our sacrifice of praise, and our sacrificial offerings. When those three are in order, fire will be falling from heaven upon the altar of our hearts.

"How will I know if the fire has come upon my heart?" If you have to ask, then you don't know, have never been there. When the fire falls, you can't get enough of God. You can't pray enough, praise enough or be in the house of the Lord enough. You are so motivated that when your body doesn't want to go, your spirit man makes it. When your body doesn't want to pray your spirit man says, *"Get out of bed, we are going to pray."* You fall out of bed if you have to so that you can pray.

When you have the fire, you have motivation from the inside moving on the outside and getting your flesh going. When you have the fire on the inside of you then at offering time your flesh will be saying, *"No, you are not going to give that amount."* Your spirit man says, *"Yes, I am. I am doing it. I am writing the check."* Your flesh will argue but will not win.

That is when you know you have fire. There is a motivation to pray, a motivation to be in the house of God. There is hunger that is a burning desire, a zeal for God.

Someone who does not have the fire will think that the rest of us are crazy because they can't understand it. It takes someone who is in the fire to understand someone else who is in the fire. It is hard to have fellowship with someone who is not in the fire because there is not a lot to talk about. All you want to talk about is God, the revelation of the Word, His presence, His goodness, and His mercy.

God sends the fire because of prayer and sacrifice. If you have neither one of those things going on in your life, there will be no fire.

Once you have developed your house into a house of prayer and a house of sacrifice then God makes your house a house of fire. Remember, fire is the passion for God. If you have enough fire of God in you then you will not only have the passion for God but you will begin to develop the passion of God. When you have the passion of God, you are consumed with the fire of God. The passion of God is to win the world to Himself. You will want to go to the nations. You will want to go to your neighbor. You will find everybody you can and get them into the kingdom of God. You want everybody to know how wonderful God is.

If you stay in the fire by staying in prayer and staying in sacrifice God will release glory. Then you will become a house of glory.

2 Chronicles 7:1-3; *"Now when Solomon had made an end of praying, the fire came down from heaven, and consumed the burnt offering and the sacrifices; and the glory of the LORD filled the house. And the priests could not enter into the house of the LORD, because the glory of the LORD had filled the LORD'S house. And when all the children of*

Israel saw how the fire came down, and the glory of the LORD upon the house, they bowed themselves with their faces to the ground upon the pavement, and worshipped, and praised the LORD, saying, For he is good; for his mercy endureth for ever."

The offerings and the sacrifices were on the altar before the fire came down. Solomon had been praying.

After the fire came down, the glory <u>filled</u> the house. "*Glory*" comes from the word *kawbod*. It literally means the weightiest matter about God, meaning His personality, His character, and His nature. When we say that the glory of God filled the house, we could say that God Himself filled the house.

When you are walking around filled with the glory of God then the very things that makes Him God is inside of you. Signs, wonders and miracles will accompany the individual who has the fullness of God in their life.

Anointing is the hand of God to remove yokes, destroy burdens and set people free. Jesus went around healing all who were oppressed of the devil.[27] Healing and deliverance are the job of the anointing. Signs, wonders and miracles (including creative miracles) can never be done by the anointing.

Only the glory of God can produce signs, wonders and miracles. We have used John 2:11 to show this.

John 2:11; *"This beginning of miracles did Jesus in Cana of Galilee, and manifested forth his glory"*

Anointing did not turn the water into wine. Glory did. The raising of the dead is not done by anointing. It is done by glory.[28] The anointing has limitations. The glory doesn't because it is God Himself.

---

[27] Acts 10:38
[28] John 11:40

Love is an attribute of God's personality. Paul spoke in Ephesians about knowing the length and the depth and the breath and the height of the love of Christ.

Ephesians 3:18-20; *"May be able to comprehend with all saints what is the breadth, and length, and depth, and height; And to know the love of Christ, which passeth knowledge, that ye might be filled with all the fulness of God. Now unto him that is able to do exceeding abundantly above all that we ask or think, according to the power that worketh in us,"*

The power Paul was talking about was glory. Anointing is limited; glory is unlimited. Anointing is done through the hands of man. Glory is done by God. When the glory fills a place, man doesn't have to do anything. It will be done by God Himself.

In services when God begins to fill teeth, I am not laying hands on the people until after it is actually happening. It is glory. God is doing it. Anointing takes man and God together. God does the glory. He may have a man speak a word or pray a prayer but it will be God Himself activating things.

Anointing is a deposit of power that we use. We don't use the glory. The glory uses us. The glory does what He wants to do because He is the glory.

Isaiah 60:7b; *"I will glorify the house of my glory."*

God was talking about us. We are supposed to be houses of glory. God wants to glorify His house of glory and it ties in with fasting and prayer. Fasting and prayer will help you position yourself to become a house of glory just like sacrificial giving does. Fasting is a sacrifice.

The armor of God covers everything but your backside. The armor is the anointing. Through fasting and prayer, which is sacrifice and praise, the Lord will be your rear guard. Rear guard means rear protection. His glory will surround you and protect even the vulnerable parts of your life.

Isaiah 58:8; *"The glory of the Lord shall be your rear guard."* **(NKJV)**

What the anointing won't do, He will. The glory will make the weak areas strong. Are you ready for God to do some things you cannot do? When you are ready, He will take over, do what you cannot and that is the glory.

Did you know that if you have the glory of God, you have the favor of God? That means what God has called you to do will start happening. God will make it happen if His glory is with you. His glory will cause people to hook up with you. Some people never have gone anywhere in their ministry because they were trying to operate on the anointing. They never went into the glory. They can lay hands on the sick and see some people get saved but no one is hooking up with their vision. The reason is because they have no glory. The glory will cause people to hook up with you. The scripture for this is found in Isaiah.

The Lord says that He is going to cause people to come to the brightness of your rising. That chapter continues to say that they shall come from afar. They will come by land, by sea and by air. They will be nourished by your side and will release the forces of the Gentiles (meaning the wealth) into your hands. Somebody is going to hook up with you when they see the glory on you.

If you have a vision from God then that vision is so big you can't do it by yourself. That tells me that you are going to have to have people for your life and God is going to have to send them.[29] Isaiah says they won't come until they see the brightness of your rising, the glory of the Lord upon you. And we thought all we needed was the anointing. No, we have to have the glory of God. The glory of God will cause people to see what God has destined you to be and they will want to be a part of it. Are you beginning to see how what God told you is going to get off the ground? Even sinners will hook up with you when they see the glory. They will get saved and want to fund your ministry.

---

[29] Isaiah 43:4

"Well, I have a vision to go to other countries but I don't have any money." You need glory. If you have glory, people will hook up with your vision and help fund it.

I challenge you to read Isaiah 60:1-11 prayerfully. Ask God to open your eyes. Do word studies. For example, did you know that the word *"forces"* there means wealth of the Gentiles? Study it verse by verse, word by word. When you get through you will want the glory and ask God for it. He will respond by saying, *"House of prayer, house of sacrifice. Then I will send my fire followed by my glory."*

We want the blessings of God but are we willing to follow the pattern that gets it? If we want Bible results, we have to follow Bible steps and examples. When we read the book of Acts, we want the miracles they did. But, are we willing to do what they did to have the miracles they had? God is not a respecter of persons but He is a respecter of faith and a respecter of dedication. He is a respecter of prayer and a respecter of sacrifice.

"Why is God blessing so-and-so so much?" Because He is a respecter of their faith, their actions, their obedience and their dedication.

Let's look at what happened to Solomon that took him into the success of his ministry. With glory you get God, which means you get His wisdom, His knowledge, His understanding and His capabilities. Talk about no limitation any more.

Did you know that is why Adam could name all the different species of animals and insects and remember what he had named them? He had the glory on himself. When he sinned, the glory lifted and he was naked. The glory is a garment. He had the wisdom of the ages and the ability of Almighty God when he had the glory.

2 Chronicles 1:6; *"And Solomon went up thither to the brasen altar before the LORD, which was at the tabernacle of the congregation, and offered a thousand burnt offerings upon it."*

When you study this you will see burnt offerings meant that God burned them. God sent the fire.

2 Chronicles 1:7; *"In that night did God appear unto Solomon"*

That is glory. Glory means that God Himself has come down. The Ark of the Covenant was called the glory of God because it represented God being there in person.

2 Chronicles 1:7; *"In that night did God appear unto Solomon, and said unto him, Ask what I shall give thee."*

Solomon offers a thousand bullocks. God sends down the fire to consume them. Next God sends His glory by showing up in person and saying, *"Ask what I shall give thee."*

2 Chronicles 1:10; *"Give me now wisdom and knowledge, that I may go out and come in before this people: for who can judge this thy people, that is so great?"*

2 Chronicles 1:12; *"Wisdom and knowledge is granted unto thee; and I will give thee riches, and wealth, and honour, such as none of the kings have had that have been before thee, neither shall there any after thee have the like."*

Glory is not limited. It can give you anything. There is no limitation because glory is God Himself.

God is looking for a heart that wants Him more than life itself.

Moses is the one who really helped us understand God. He asked God to show His glory.[30] The Lord showed His glory by showing him His goodness, His name, His mercy, His grace. All of those are the nature of God.

---

[30] Exodus 33:18-19

Moses went before Pharaoh more than one time asking that the people be allowed to leave. Pharaoh wanted to enter the compromise zone. Moses said they couldn't do that. It would be an abomination to all the other gods the Egyptians worshiped. It would make Pharaoh angry and he would want to kill the Israelites for it.

Moses told him that they could not sacrifice and serve God in bondage. That is also why we need deliverance.

Pharaoh came back and said that only the men could go. Moses did not agree with that either. They all needed to go. Don't accept the compromises of the enemy. *"Well, you are a Christian so don't expect your family to become one."* Wrong, you tell the devil that you are all coming out of bondage.

Pharaoh tried one more time to compromise. Yes, they could go but leave everything behind. Moses again said, *"No, we have to take everything with us. We do not know what our God may require as a sacrifice."* That was wisdom.

When it comes to sacrifice it is not up to us to dictate. With offerings, you can go from your heart. But sacrifice, God will ask. It is called a requirement. God told Abraham what to offer – his son Isaac. With a sacrifice, God is in charge. With an offering, we are.

Offering would be connected to anointing, sacrifice to glory. That is why few Christians have the glory of God and many of them have the anointing. They can get some people delivered, get some healed but when it comes to creative miracles few Christians flow in it. It requires more than the average Christian is willing to give.

We have to be willing to enter the realms of prayer and of sacrifice. We must pray that God's will be done in and through each one of us. And then we must do it in order to have the glory of God manifest in our lives.

Made in the USA
Columbia, SC
07 October 2020